Young Royals on Tour

Young Royals on Tour

William & Catherine in Canada

CHRISTINA BLIZZARD

DUNDURN

TORONTO

Editors: Allister Thompson and Michael Carroll
Design: Jennifer Scott

Library and Archives Canada Cataloguing in Publication

Blizzard, Christina, 1948-
    Young royals on tour : William & Catherine in Canada / by Christina Blizzard.

Issued also in electronic formats.
ISBN 978-1-4597-0186-1

1. William, Prince, grandson of Elizabeth II, Queen of Great Britain, 1982-. 2. Middleton, Kate, 1982-. 3. Royal visitors--Canada. 4. Princes--Great Britain. 5. Princesses--Great Britain. I. Title.

FC223.R6 2011 B55 2011   971.07'3   C2011-902870-0

1 2 3 4 5   15 14 13 12 11

Conseil des Arts du Canada — Canada Council for the Arts   Canadä   ONTARIO ARTS COUNCIL / CONSEIL DES ARTS DE L'ONTARIO

We acknowledge the support of the **Canada Council for the Arts** and the **Ontario Arts Council** for our publishing program. We also acknowledge the financial support of the **Government of Canada** through the **Canada Book Fund** and **Livres Canada Books**, and the **Government of Ontario** through the **Ontario Book Publishing Tax Credit** and the **Ontario Media Development Corporation**.

Care has been taken to trace the ownership of copyright material used in this book. The author and the publisher welcome any information enabling them to rectify any references or credits in subsequent editions.

J. Kirk Howard, President

Printed and bound in Canada.
www.dundurn.com

Dundurn	Gazelle Book Services Limited	Dundurn
3 Church Street, Suite 500	White Cross Mills	2250 Military Road
Toronto, Ontario, Canada	High Town, Lancaster, England	Tonawanda, NY
M5E 1M2	LA1 4XS	U.S.A. 14150

CONTENTS

INTRODUCTION:
Royal Newlyweds Wowed Canada

The world fell in love with William and Catherine when they wed, and Canada was the first country to welcome them as they kicked off their first state visit. Will 'n Kate fever swept the country, starting on June 30, 2011. The newly minted Duke and Duchess of Cambridge began their nine-day tour at Rideau Hall in Ottawa followed by Canada Day festivities in the nation's capital.

What better way to greet the young man — who may one day be Canada's King — and his new bride? It didn't matter who you were or where you were from. If you were in Ottawa on Canada Day 2011, you were Canadian.

The itinerary was inspired and touched many cornerstones of Canadian society — young people, aboriginal groups, and the military. It was geographically diverse, with stops in Quebec, Prince Edward Island, Alberta, and the Northwest Territories. In La Belle Province they visited both Montreal and Quebec City, gestures guaranteed to raise the popularity of the monarchy in a part of the country that isn't a traditional bastion of royal support.

Westminster Abbey

London, England's Westminster Abbey is one of the most famous buildings in the world, but in its long history surprisingly few royal weddings have taken place there. The first was in 1100, and the hallowed abbey has been used sparingly for that purpose in subsequent centuries. There were only nine royal weddings at Westminster in the twentieth century, including the 1986 marriage of Prince Andrew to Sarah Ferguson, and the marriages of the Queen's daughter, Princess Anne, in 1973 and that of the Queen's sister, Princess Margaret, in 1960. Queen Elizabeth II herself was married there in 1947.

Catherine seems a smart, media-savvy young woman, and this tour was her first test. William's great-grandmother, the Queen Mother, loved Canada and Canadians, and always had the right word at the right time. She could melt the sternest of republican hearts. Her husband, George VI, was the first reigning monarch to tour Canada. In 1939 they arrived in Quebec. Asked whether she was English or Scottish, the Queen Mother famously replied: "Since we reached Quebec, I've been Canadian."

Buckingham Palace is no doubt hoping Catherine has those same instincts. She and William bring a fresh, modern face to the monarchy.

Canada rolled out the red-and-white carpet and showed William and Catherine what a right royal Canadian welcome looks like!

DAY ONE:
Arrival in Ottawa

The Newlyweds Dazzled at Their Coming-Out Party

Okay, the answer to your most pressing questions. Yes, William is tall and handsome — and very personable. And Kate is slim — she looks thinner even than on her wedding day. And she waded into the whole royal walkabout thing as if she had been doing it all her life. Most important, what strikes you about this young couple is that they are the genuine article.

The first stop on their nine-day Canadian tour was at the National War Memorial where they spent so long talking to veterans and their families that they put their tour schedule into a tailspin. The couple didn't just shake hands and exchange a few pleasantries. They chatted intensely at times with people who had waited for hours to catch a glimpse of the royal newlyweds. Ottawa's Lois Mullins was one of them. She planted her chair at the memorial at 8:30 a.m. for the 2:30 p.m. meet-and-greet.

"I am the same age as the Queen, and our husbands are the same age, and we got married the same year, and our boys were born the same year," she said.

Later, at Rideau Hall, the residence of Canada's governor general, two youngsters from Pembroke, Ontario, donned fashionable fascinators and greeted their favourite Royals. Elizabeth Webster, nine, and Charlotte Oattes, eleven, wanted to see William and Catherine because they had watched the royal wedding.

"We wanted to see them in real life and so did my mom," said Elizabeth.

William thrilled the crowd by speaking first in French. The throng cheered, and he joked that his French "will get better as we go along."

He told everyone he and Catherine had been "longing" to come to Canada for years. "The geography of Canada is unsurpassed and is famous for being matched only by the hospitality of its people," he said.

> **The Tour Theme**
>
> The theme of the 2011 Royal Tour was "Moving Forward Together: From Past Accomplishments to Current Service to Future Achievements." The title emphasizes both the rich history of the Crown in Canada as well as the potential of the institution to make future contributions to Canadian identity and Commonwealth relations. The royal couple represents a newer, more modern aspect to the monarchy that will reach out to coming generations.

The royal couple lays a wreath at the National War Memorial.

Even Prime Minister Stephen Harper was in a playful mood as he joked about how disappointed he and his wife, Laureen, were that they hadn't been able to attend the royal wedding because of the recent federal election.

It was a right royal start, and these two young people did themselves proud.

Don't forget that Catherine is new to all this. She isn't used to pomp and circumstance, so this tour was a greater test for her than it was for William, who is used to being in the public eye.

Still, Catherine managed to get off to a flying start fashion-wise, wearing not just one but two Canadian designers — Smythe and Erdem — on her first day. She wore one outfit to get on the plane, then changed into another aboard the Canadian Forces Airbus.

Height of Fashion

Travelling to Canada, the Duchess of Cambridge showed how adept she was in her diplomatic role, with a blazer by Toronto label Smythe les Vestes, paired over a sheath by French label Roland Mouret. Smythe, known for its beautifully fitted blazers and coats that aren't only designed but also made in Canada, was a good choice for Catherine, whose coat collection was already the envy of women the world over.

Sometime during the overseas flight, Catherine traded in her navy suit for a lovely dress that was perhaps more suited to the warmer Canadian weather. The lacy ensemble, worn with a discreet slip, seemed appropriate for her arrival in Canada.

The "Cecile" dress was created by Erdem Moralioğlu, a designer originally from Montreal who has set up shop in the United Kingdom to much acclaim. The navy dress featured a beautiful intricate pattern, with abstract leaf and petal motifs interwoven throughout. The navy tones were an appropriate hue, considering the couple's first stop was Ottawa's War Memorial.

— *With files from Rebecca Zamon*

The Duchess of Cambridge, wearing her "Cecile" dress, greets a young fan in Ottawa.

A Rapturous Welcome

The British media extensively covered the first stop on the Canadian tour. Gordon Raynor of the *Telegraph* wrote: "Thousands of people cheered Catherine's every step of the way as she went on a walkabout in the centre of Ottawa, and many of them chanted her name rock star style."

Roya Nikkhah described how William and Catherine relaxed and had fun taking in the evening Canada Day show on Parliament Hill. "After two days of official ceremonies, handshakes, gun salutes, and carefully managed walkabouts, the Duke and Duchess of Cambridge got into the party spirit on Friday night, attending a pop concert for the finale of the Canada Day celebrations, marking the country's 144th birthday."

—*With files from Scott Taylor*

Above left: This sheet music was printed to commemorate Queen Elizabeth II's first Canadian tour in 1951 when she was still Princess Elizabeth.

Above right: Diana enjoyed Niagara Falls with William and Harry in 1991.

Left: Catherine speaks with flower girls at Rideau Hall on June 30.

Above: The Duke and Duchess stand with Prime Minister Harper and his wife.

William and Catherine were clearly working hard and doing their best to make a good impression, and they were off to a grand start.

The next day, on the nation's birthday, they would take part in a swearing-in ceremony for new Canadians and were scheduled to be on Parliament Hill for the biggest birthday bash Ottawa would ever see. Hundreds of thousands of people were expected to arrive from all over southern Ontario for the noontime show.

Little Maria Aragon, who astonished Lady Gaga with her version of "Born This Way," would sing the national anthem, and Great Big Sea and the Sam Roberts Band were also slated to perform.

One thing was certain. It would be a royal treat.

DAY TWO:
Canada Day in Ottawa

William's Poignant Speech Was a High Point

Any royal tour comes with its share of grand moments. Words that inspire, that touch your heart when they speak of history and service and honour — and the enormous contribution of Canada's armed forces in so many conflicts around the world for so many years.

And there was all that on July 1 on Parliament Hill.

Canada Day had two special guests — the Duke and Duchess of Cambridge. Ottawa was awash in red and white as hundreds of thousands of jubilant well-wishers jammed the Hill and neighbouring streets. William gave a short but poignant speech. He talked about how Catherine had learned of Canada from her grandfather, who had trained as a pilot in Alberta.

You couldn't help remembering as he spoke of his Canadian family that Friday would have been the fiftieth birthday of his mother, Diana.

In 1991 Diana sailed with Prince William and Prince Harry on the HMY *Britannia*. Canada Day 2011 would have been her fiftieth birthday.

Canada Day

The royal couple aren't the first members of the Royal Family to attend July 1 Canada Day ceremonies. William's grandmother, Queen Elizabeth II, along with Prince Philip, attended the celebration in Ottawa in 2010. After being introduced by actor Christopher Plummer, speaking to the thousands of assembled Canadians on Parliament Hill, she praised the country's distinctive character and its compassionate values. Her previous most recent Canada Day appearance was in 1997.

15

Queen Elizabeth II met Canadians on Canada Day 2010 (left). The maple leaf pin that she wore was given to her by her mother, and then to Kate, who donned it for the evening's festivities on Canada Day 2011 (below).

Below left: Queen Elizabeth wore the Maple Leaf brooch during her 1951 visit.

The Duke of Cambridge hails Canadian well-wishers on Canada Day.

Party Time on Parliament Hill

Some slept on the hard ground of Parliament Hill, others arrived at the break of dawn for a Canada Day party with the royal couple. The average Canada Day crowd on Parliament Hill and throughout the downtown core is about 350,000, but this year the number had already reached 300,000 by noon.

The Duke and Duchess of Cambridge watched Governor General David Johnston inspect the royal guard before shaking hands and speaking to some in the crowd. They did the same on their walk out.

William and Catherine, along with the hundreds of thousands who packed Parliament Hill, also watched a series of performances in the two-hour show by Canadian artists. Prince William made a speech, congratulating the Canadian soldiers who have served in Afghanistan.

— *With files from Jamie Long*

Queen Elizabeth and Prince Philip opened Parliament in 1977 during the Queen's silver jubilee celebrations.

William and Catherine did an extended walkabout after the show. Some in the crowd told him they were thinking about his mother on her birthday, and he thanked them for their kindness. The heat proved too much for some, and many people fainted. As he shook hands, the Duke kept reminding people to drink lots of water.

But all eyes were on Catherine. She wore the same cream dress she had donned for her official engagement shoot, along with red court shoes and a stylish red fascinator with a maple leaf design.

"Speaking of families and of loved ones far away, this is an important moment for Canada," the Duke told the cheering crowd. "For this month the servicemen and women of the Canadian Forces cease their combat role in Afghanistan," he said. "This draws to a close an episode of which all Canadians can be immensely proud."

The Duke went on to praise Canada's military contribution in countless conflicts. "Our armed forces have always led the world in rallying to the defence of freedom. From Vimy Ridge and Juno Beach, through Korea and the Balkans to Kandahar Province, the sacrifice of Canadians has been universally revered and respected," he said.

Sometimes, though, it is the smaller gestures that touch hearts. And those were found earlier at the citizenship ceremony across the Ottawa River in Gatineau, Quebec.

Newcomers to this country found themselves shaking hands with the fairy-tale couple — the beautiful young Cinderella who had risen from (relatively) humble origins to marry her prince.

The royal couple is escorted through the crowds on Canada Day.

The Duke speaks with a new Canadian at the citizenship ceremony.

People like Siddhartha Kumar, who came here five years ago from India. He married Canadian Jacinthe Marcil in 2005, and they now make Gatineau their home.

"It's very special," he said. "Being a Canadian is special, but then to have the Royals here, I don't think it could have been better than this."

This is a very new, different kind of royalty. They're young, they're energetic, and they're engaging young people in a way that is quite remarkable. And it had only just begun. On July 2 they headed to Montreal and then to Quebec City.

They had a glorious welcome in Ottawa, but there could be heavy weather in Quebec, with some threatening protests.

New Canadians

By special invitation, twenty-five people from fourteen countries took the Oath of Citizenship on Canada Day, and what made it special was that their certificates and small Canadian flags were handed to them by the Duke and Duchess of Cambridge.

"I think the monarchy is great," said Kenneth from the Philippines. "I'm for it."

Governor General David Johnston led the twenty-five through the recital of the citizenship oath, and then one by one they went onstage to shake hands with William and Catherine, who handed them their certificates and flags.

— *With files from Earl McRae*

The Duchess of Cambridge greets the crowd after the Canadian citizenship ceremony.

DAY THREE:
Walkabout in the Nation's Capital

Catherine, Queen of the Ball

William may one day be King, but right now it seemed as if Catherine ruled in Canada.

That was the feeling after the Duke and Duchess of Cambridge wrapped up their stay in Ottawa and headed to Montreal. The royal newlyweds met and chatted with Canadian veterans and war brides at the Canadian War Museum.

Gordon Standing, ninety, flew thirty missions over Europe in the Second World War as part of 415 Squadron based in East Moor, Yorkshire. William inquired about the veteran's medals and asked Standing what his role had been in the unit.

At the tree-planting ceremony the royal couple speak with Terry Joyce, a terminally ill man whose last wish was to meet them.

21

The Duke and Duchess share a shovel during the tree-planting
ceremony at Rideau Hall.

22

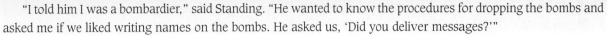

"I told him I was a bombardier," said Standing. "He wanted to know the procedures for dropping the bombs and asked me if we liked writing names on the bombs. He asked us, 'Did you deliver messages?'"

When Standing told the Duke he hadn't, he said William commented that it was "mostly an American thing. And I suggested it was."

Catherine spoke with a number of war brides, such as Marjory Berry, originally from the Shepherd's Bush area of London, England. She said Catherine made her feel "very comfortable" and chatted with her for some time about her experiences.

Captain Jeff McCartney went to naval college in Britain and served in the Pacific theatre. He also had experience in search-and-rescue missions and talked with William about a planned exercise in Prince Edward Island that would see the Duke participate in a faked crash.

William, who is in active service with the Royal Air Force's search-and-rescue arm, is interested in the way men and women of Canada's armed forces have served their country.

> **His Own Flag**
>
> William now has his own flag. When the Duke of Cambridge arrived in Ottawa, a new flag was flown to signal his arrival. It was used to indicate his presence at all locations during the royal visit. The flag's design was developed over a three-month period by the Canadian heraldic authority at Rideau Hall. It was inspired by the personal flag adopted by Queen Elizabeth II in 1962 and was approved by Her Majesty.

William's new flag was developed over a three-month period by the Canadian heraldic authority at Rideau Hall.

The royal couple chat with war brides at the Canadian War Museum in Ottawa.

The couple was greeted by cheering crowds everywhere they stopped. The charm they exuded put people at ease, and they seemed genuinely interested in people's lives.

While at the War Museum the couple also unveiled an unfinished mural by Augustus John.

Catherine continued to amaze Canadians with her grace, and everyone was in awe of how quickly she had adapted to her new life. William is used to living his life in a fishbowl, but not Catherine. She was born a commoner and is used to doing her own grocery shopping and laundry. Now, in Canada, she was shaking hands and making small talk with hundreds of people every day. And she was coping very well.

On July 2, the day after what would have been Diana's fiftieth birthday, Catherine wore a dress by Catherine Walker, Diana's favourite designer. A tribute, you couldn't help thinking, to a woman she had never known but whose memory was very much with the couple that weekend.

At the Canadian War Museum

To many royal fans the final day of William and Catherine's visit to Ottawa seemed like the best chance to meet the royal couple. But, unlike earlier public appearances on the newlyweds' first international tour, time along the barricades was very limited on July 2.

A small crowd waited outside the Canadian War Museum Saturday afternoon, underneath the scorching sun. The Duke and Duchess started Saturday with an early-afternoon tree planting on the grounds of Rideau Hall where they had stayed for two nights, and mingled briefly with the public. But William and Catherine wasted little time between arriving and entering the museum, only waving a couple of times to the crowd.

Inside they unveiled a mural and signed the museum's official guestbook. They also lingered, separating and talking to most of the veterans, war brides, and their families who attended a small reception.

— *With files from Jamie Long*

William and Catherine pose in front of the unfinished Augustus John mural at the Canadian War Museum.

DAYS THREE AND FOUR:
Return to Quebec

The Royals Sailed into Quebeckers' Hearts

The last Royal Family member to visit Montreal was Prince Charles in 2009, and that didn't go down very well. Rowdy separatist protesters made life very difficult for the Prince of Wales and his wife, Camilla. Queen Elizabeth II's last appearance in Quebec City was in 1987, and though Her Majesty's stay wasn't marred by anything remotely tumultuous or violent as was the case during her 1964 visit, her reception couldn't be described as warm and fuzzy. So some people might argue that it was pretty daring for William and Catherine to include Montreal and Quebec City in their nine-day tour of Canada.

Jeering separatist protesters did materialize near Sainte-Justine University Hospital in Montreal where the Duke and Duchess of Cambridge paid a visit to the cancer and neonatal units on July 2, but their catcalls and banging of tin drums were largely drowned out by the enthusiastic cheers of a much larger assembly of well-wishers. While in the hospital, William and Catherine talked to four young children with blood diseases or cancer. The Duchess congratulated one boy on his artwork, and William told them to be strong.

Later during their time in Montreal, William and Catherine attended a culinary class at the Institut de tourisme et d'hôtelier du Québec. The royal couple donned the same white chef's

Left: Queen Elizabeth II rides the monorail at Expo 67 in Montreal.

Facing: The Duke and Duchess disembark from HMCS *Montréal* after arriving in Quebec City.

Queen Elizabeth II and Quebec

Despite the sometimes controversial history of Quebec's relationship with the rest of Canada and with the monarchy, Queen Elizabeth II has visited the province a number of times. In 1955 she was presented with the puck with which Maurice "Rocket" Richard scored his 325th goal. She visited the province in 1957 and attended Montreal's Expo 67, a high point in the nation's history. While the Queen cherishes Quebec's distinct society and rich role in Canada's history, she is also a great supporter of federalism, a point made again by a visit to Quebec City in 1987. William and Catherine's visit once again emphasizes the royal family's commitment to Quebec's role in a united Canada.

William shakes hands with children in military garb in Lévis, outside Quebec City.

jackets as the students, sans chef hats, and assisted in the preparation of a meal that they shared with Quebec Premier Jean Charest and his wife, Michele.

That evening William and Catherine got onboard the frigate HMCS *Montréal* for an overnight cruise on the St. Lawrence River to Quebec City. The ship was dubbed the "Love Boat" for this romantic voyage by the newlyweds.

Or should that be *Bateau d'Amour*?

There was a prayer service aboard HMCS *Montréal* first thing in the morning when the frigate docked in Quebec's capital. One of the guests was local Huron Chief Konrad Sioui. He sported a magnificent traditional headpiece made of turkey and eagle feathers, which the Duchess, who has remarkably good taste in headgear herself, admired. More important, though, he had brought along for the Duke a copy of a treaty signed by a Huron grand chief and King George III in 1760, promising the two communities would live side by side in peace.

"Two hundred and thirty years later the message of that treaty is still intact and that relationship shall be that we shall live as brothers, not as father and son," Sioui said.

The royal couple responds to the warm reception by their fans in Lévis.

This is a very traditional response of First Nations to Royals. They like to deal directly with the Queen as the descendant of the person who signed their original treaty nation to nation.

One day William will likely be King, so it was important for Sioui to keep that continuity alive. "You represent what is the essence of Canada," Sioui told the Duke.

He was exactly right. William — and Catherine — represent the start of a new relationship between Canada and the monarchy.

The Royals understand this relationship with Canada's aboriginal people. They understand it better than do many Canadian politicians. In Newfoundland many years ago the Queen went over to shake the hands of Native protesters when politicians tried to give them a wide berth.

There had been demonstrations threatened in the heartland of Quebec nationalism, and certainly there was noise and there was shouting, but the demonstrators were kept well away from the Duke and Duchess of Cambridge. And they were far outnumbered by the thousands of people who turned out to catch a glimpse of the royal couple.

Right: These admirers from New Brunswick travelled to Quebec to see the royal couple.

Below: Catherine meets and greets in Quebec City.

The Duke meets with Konrad Sioui, grand chief of the Huron Tribe of Amer-Indians, after attending a morning service in Quebec City onboard the HMCS *Montréal*.

In short, everything was civilized. No Vancouver hockey riots here. Although security was tight, with sniffer dogs and sharpshooters on roofs. The protesters got to be heard, and those who came out to see the Royals were treated to some fine pageantry.

Let's face it. A lot of the people were there not so much to support the monarchy as to see this lovely young couple who are on top of the double-A celebrity list.

There was very little interaction between the royal couple and citizens in Montreal, but Quebec City was a different matter. At City Hall William and Catherine even went up to the barricades to shake hands, allow photographs to be snapped, and speak with the happily whooping multitude.

The Duke and Duchess joined Premier Charest and Régis Labeaume, mayor of Quebec City, on the steps of City Hall, where William reviewed members of the 2nd Battalion of the Royal 22nd Regiment — the famed Van Doos — who have served Canada in so many conflicts, most recently in Afghanistan. The soldiers were resplendent in their red dress uniforms and had their goat mascot on hand, as well.

The Duke inspects the honour guard in Quebec City.

William and Catherine were at City Hall to commemorate the 403rd birthday of Quebec City and to take part in the Freedom of the City ceremony, which dates back to 1748 when fortified towns only allowed armies known to be friendly to enter their gates.

The Duke gave a short speech, all in French. He apologized for his accent, but the good-natured crowd just laughed at his joke — and applauded him.

Good for him. And good for Catherine. It took courage to come to a place where protests were promised. These two young people carried their visit off with grace and elegance beyond their years.

DAY FIVE:
The Duke and Duchess Amazed Prince Edward Island

An Action-Packed Day in P.E.I.

July 4 saw William and Catherine take part in a wide range of hands-on activities. It seemed as if the whole of Prince Edward Island turned out to see the royal pair at Province House in Charlottetown where Canada had become a nation. Islanders, it appeared, just couldn't get enough of the Duke and Duchess of Cambridge.

Premier Robert Ghiz had some advice for William. Ghiz — whose wife's name is also Kate — warned William to remember that "Kates are always right."

Simulating engine failure while landing a Sikorsky C-124 Sea King helicopter on water is called "waterbirding." It is a classic Canadian technique used to train pilots who might actually experience such a calamity. Only a handful of U.K. pilots have been trained in the procedure, so when William, a flight lieutenant, returned to his Royal Air Force detachment in Wales, he took back with him some uniquely Canadian skills.

Major Patrick MacNamara, commanding officer of the Helicopter Test and Evaluation Centre in Shearwater, Nova Scotia, was the navigator in the helicopter with

Green, Green Island

The tour stop in Prince Edward Island was designed to highlight Prince Edward Island's natural beauty, historical significance, and cultural traditions. "The tour is a wonderful opportunity to shine the spotlight on Prince Edward Island and offer Their Royal Highnesses an authentic look at our province," stated Premier Robert Ghiz in a press release. "We will showcase Prince Edward Island's rich history and various cultures, traditions, artistic talent, and innovative products." Kate Macdonald Butler, the granddaughter of Lucy Maud Montgomery, author of *Anne of Green Gables*, presented the Duchess of Cambridge with the 100th anniversary edition of the book Catherine is reported to have loved as a child.

Left: The Duke and Duchess of Cambridge meet admirers in Charlottetown after touching down at the airport.

Below: Catherine receives a bouquet upon arrival in Prince Edward Island.

East Coast Fashion

One part nautical, the other part nostalgic, Catherine, Duchess of Cambridge, greeted the East Coast of Canada with a lighter touch to her ensemble.

She wore a cream-coloured cable-knit sweater dress with a drop waist complete with blue stripes around the hem, waistline, and wrists, finishing the look with an artfully tied collar hanging in a sailor's knot around her neck. It was a new style in white tones with a designer the Duchess was quite familiar with — Sarah Burton for Alexander McQueen, the creator of her famed wedding gown.

The crowds in Charlottetown undoubtedly loved this homage to their maritime heritage, and with her hair tied back prettily in a ponytail, Catherine seemed ready for a day full of adventure.
— *With files from Rebecca Zamon*

Prince William takes the controls of a Canadian Forces Sea King helicopter at Dalvay-by-the-Sea during his "waterbirding" manoeuvre.

William at Dalvay-by-the-Sea. "He [the Duke] was fantastic actually," MacNamara told reporters afterward. "He was very crisp in all his manoeuvres."

William didn't just perform the task once. He spent almost an hour in the aircraft, wipers clearing spray from the windscreen as he executed the tricky operation that occasionally caused the water level to surge toward the windows. It seemed as if he was having fun. Perhaps, though, that's what search-and-rescue pilots do for relaxation.

What struck everyone most about the young Royals was that they were trying so hard. The weather was wet and cold on July 4, but earlier in Charlottetown, Catherine refused the offer of an umbrella as she got into an open landau for a procession down the provincial capital's Great George Street. Clearly, she wanted the crowds to get a good view and not be disappointed.

After the waterbirding demonstration, the couple competed in a dragon boat race on Dalvay Lake. Catherine and William paddled in different dragon boats. The Duchess, decked out in black sportswear, took the stern of her craft. She

---

Lucy Maud Montgomery's Royal Connection

The novels and journals of the author of *Anne of Green Gables* are thick with references to matters and people royal, including a mention in *Anne's House of Dreams* to the visit of the Prince of Wales (later King Edward VII) to Charlottetown in 1860. As recorded in her journal in 1901, Lucy Maud Montgomery joined royal watchers in Halifax, Nova Scotia, to greet the Duke of York (later King George V), who was touring the British Empire with his wife, the Duchess of York, who would one day be Queen Mary. More than two decades later, on August 6, 1927, Montgomery met the Prince of Wales and his brother, Prince George, at a garden party at Government House in Toronto. Eight years later the Prince of Wales ascended the throne briefly as Edward VIII. His brother, Prince George (later Duke of Kent), was killed in an airplane crash in Scotland en route to Iceland and then bound to Newfoundland. The gloves Montgomery was wearing when she shook hands with the Prince of Wales were kept as cherished heirlooms.

The Duke and Duchess compete in a dragon boat race on different teams. William's boat won the race.

Dragon Boats

Boston Bruins defenceman Adam McQuaid went from winning the Stanley Cup to losing bragging rights in a royal dragon boat race. The twenty-four-year-old Charlottetowner rowed on Catherine's team as she went head-to-head with William in a race on a rainy lake. Even with the help of the six-foot-four Bruin, the Duchess didn't win the race. Her team lost by a head.

Still, McQuaid got a kick out of getting the invitation to row on the team. "I found out almost the day after we won the Stanley Cup that they wanted me to be part of this — so much going on, so much excitement," he said.

Despite being a prince, William promised there would be no chivalry during the race. "William was joking around, giving us the thumbs-down, booing when we were getting started," McQuaid said.

— With files from Jessica Murphy

had an expected edge over her husband, since she had been part of a dragon boat crew in 2007. However, the Duke's vessel won, and when he reached the dock, he wrapped his arm around his wife in a seemingly tender embrace. In response she nudged him as if to topple him into the water.

"There's no chivalry in sport," the Duke joked as he was awarded a bottle of champagne to mark his victory.

Catherine laughed and said, "Sadly, we lost."

The newlyweds were then welcomed with a traditional Mi'kmaq "smudging" ceremony, followed by performances by step dancers, Mi'kmaq entertainers, and popular island singer Meaghan Blanchard and her band. Blanchard suffered some embarrassment when she called William "Dootch" instead of Duke, a gaffe that inspired laughter on the part of the royal couple and led to Catherine playfully slapping her husband on the shoulder.

At one point the newlyweds were presented with samples of P.E.I. food. William mock-held his hands to his stomach and ruefully joked about eating too much on the tour. When the royal couple was offered some oysters, William said to Catherine, "This is where you take over."

William and Catherine participate in a traditional Mi'kmaq "smudging" ceremony at Dalvay-by-the-Sea.

Above: The royal couple arrives for the events at Dalvay-by-the-Sea.

Left: Catherine has a laugh at the beach events.

Below: The Duchess of Cambridge examines some elaborate sand art on the beach at Dalvay-by-the-Sea.

Canadian Assistants

The Canadian Secretary to the Queen is the senior operational member of the Royal Household in Canada. The Secretary is responsible for communication between the Queen and the federal and provincial Canadian governments. He or she is also responsible for the official program of royal tours in Canada. The Canadian Secretary also drafts speeches that the Royals deliver. Since April 1, 2009, the Canadian Secretary has been Kevin S. MacLeod. Each member of the Royal Family has an equerry appointed to him or her for a royal tour. The equerry is a military officer who takes care of the needs of the royal member in his or her charge. Equerries greet Royal Family members in the morning and are the last to wish them good night.

Prince William, later King William IV, was the first royal visitor to Canada in 1786.

William, First Royal Visitor to Canada

The first member of the Royal Family to visit Canada was the Duke of Cambridge's namesake, Prince William (later King William IV), in 1786. A British naval officer during the Revolutionary War, he commanded a ship that travelled to Nova Scotia and Newfoundland. He returned in 1788. King William left an indelible mark on early Canada as evidenced by such place names as Prince William in New Brunswick, Williamsburg in Ontario, and King William Island in Nunavut. He also gave the royal charters for the founding of such institutions as Victoria College in Toronto.

DAY SIX:
Magic in the Land of the Midnight Sun

William Faced Off in Far North Shinny

Memo to the Duchess of Cambridge: in Canada, custom dictates you do not wear high-heeled shoes and a cream linen shift by Danish high street designer Malene Birger to a street hockey game.

Similarly, to the Duke of Cambridge: it is a big no-no to wear a business suit and tie when you're going to take shots on goal in a game of shinny.

In a competition against Northwest Territories Premier Floyd Roland, William was shut down by goalie Calvin Loman, who blocked the first two shots. The third ricocheted into a news cameraman.

Catherine was asked to join the scrimmage by teenager Gloria Francis. The Duchess pointed to her stilettos and said she couldn't play. Catherine told Gloria, sixteen, that she had played field hockey, so she had a fair idea how the sport was played. Instead, the Duchess dropped the ball for the faceoff.

Prince Charles during his first visit to the Northwest Territories in 1970.

The Royal Family in the Arctic

In 1970 Queen Elizabeth visited Manitoba and the Northwest Territories (including some areas that are now part of Nunavut), accompanied by Prince Charles and Princess Anne. That year marked the young Prince of Wales's first trip to Canada. During his tour, Charles sampled local trout, visited Native reserves, was entertained by aboriginal dancers, and met with war veterans. The Royals also witnessed a rodeo at Swan Lake, Manitoba. The Prince of Wales returned to what is now Nunavut in 1975 on a solo tour, during which he took a dive under the ice in Resolute Bay.

The royal couple arrives in Yellowknife.

A Smaller Party

William and Catherine brought seven staff members, less than has been the custom on previous tours. This is in keeping with the less lavish, more streamlined, and modern style they have assumed thus far. The team included personal hairstylist James Pryce, a private secretary, an assistant secretary, a press secretary, an administrative assistant, and Sir David Manning, a royal adviser who helped coach Catherine in the ways of royal duties to prepare her for joining the family as the Duchess of Cambridge. Catherine decided to plan her own fashions for this trip, another innovation.

"She's really beautiful and really laid-back," said the young hockey player. "She's really normal and not too much older than me. I think she would be a person I could get along with."

And if it hadn't been for those darned shoes, she would have joined in, Catherine told Gloria.

In Yellowknife, which has a large aboriginal population, William and Catherine made it a priority to pay attention to children. They spent time talking to the young hockey players, then moved on to a youth parliament where young people told them how they would change things to keep Native kids in school. Only 15.4 percent of aboriginal teens graduate from high school, while a mere 4.6 percent get university degrees.

The Duke and Duchess are presented with personalized hockey jerseys.

Above: William tries his hand at street hockey — good form, but no goals scored.

Left: The Duke addresses the crowd and dignitaries.

Catherine looks radiant under the northern sun.

Northern Fashion

In Yellowknife Catherine took another simple fashion spin. She wore a cream shift with a broad shoulder shape and touches of green, notably in a large band around her waist. The dress by Danish designer Malene Birger complemented William's dark navy suit, proving the pair's sartorial symmetry yet again. This attire gave a heightened sense of formality to the Duke and Duchess's introduction to Canada's North, which included presentations of drumming, dancing, and of course, a street hockey game. Birger is known for the particularly feminine shapes to her clothing, using the 1950s and 1960s as inspiration for dresses and fitted shirts.

— *With files from Rebecca Zamon*

A huge crowd of about three thousand turned out to welcome the royal couple. Children arrived in their Sunday-best clothes, clutching bouquets of flowers for Catherine. She stopped and chatted with them, then thanked them for coming out.

After impressing everyone with his French earlier on the tour, the Duke tested his linguistic skills further, addressing the assembled in Dene and Inuvialuktun, two of the eleven official languages of the Northwest Territories.

"The fact that he made the attempt was a very nice touch," said Northwest Territories Premier Floyd Roland of the Dene *marsi* or *thank you* that capped off William's address.

Dene National Chief Bill Erasmus said the royal acknowledgement of the First Nations people was an important one. "This is our homeland ... our culture, language, and people are alive."

The Duke complimented the Northwest Territories as an example of Canada's finest qualities in its beauty and friendliness. "It's great to be north of sixty," he said.

The couple was presented with Canadian Olympic hockey sweaters with Cambridge 1 and 2 on the back (Catherine got 1).

"Put them on!" chanted the onlookers. "Put them on!" In the end the royal couple didn't don the jerseys. It was warm and, well, they would have seemed a bit silly over the business suit and Malene Birger. And those high heels.

The Royals were later presented with amazing all-Canadian bling. Roland gave them some Harry Winston diamonds, cufflinks for William and a brooch for Catherine. All told there were 692 diamonds in the polar-bear-shaped jewellery, crafted to look like Native beadwork.

Above: A young man demonstrates a popular Inuit kicking game.

Left: William and Catherine watch a woman prepare caribou meat for smoking while visiting Blachford Lake.

45

The Duke and Duchess chat with members of the First Canadian Ranger Patrol Group at Blachford Lake.

Later the Duke and Duchess were flown to Blachford Lake where they met with the First Canadian Ranger Patrol Group, part-time reserve soldiers who conduct surveillance and sovereignty patrols in the Far North. While at Blachford Lake, they chatted with elders and students and witnessed Native dancing and games, "highlighting their unique and innovative educational program that integrates elements of traditional aboriginal knowledge and learning into a university-accredited program." The couple also enjoyed northern delicacies such as Arctic char.

Everyone was in a good mood. Even the British journalists on the tour got into the spirit of the occasion. When it turned out journalists had been positioned in front of well-wishers, the journalists helped out by snapping pictures for the locals.

An adage from another century stated that the sun never set on the British Empire. At that time Britain ruled so many countries around the world that, literally, the sun was always shining someplace where they ruled.

In the Land of the Midnight Sun where daylight lasts almost twenty-four hours a day in the summer, the warm glow from William and Catherine's visit will undoubtedly keep fond memories of the future King and his bride shining for years to come.

Anniversaries

Many royal tours have been timed to coincide with important anniversaries in Canadian history. In 1964 Queen Elizabeth II commemorated the Charlottetown and Quebec Conferences by visiting those cities. The Queen was also on hand for the centennial of Confederation in 1967. She toured Manitoba in 1970 to celebrate the centennial of that province's entry into Confederation, and attended similar ceremonies in the Northwest Territories (1970), British Columbia (1971), Prince Edward Island (1973), and Alberta and Saskatchewan (2005). Prince Charles has helped commemorate events such as the 200th anniversary of the United Empire Loyalists' arrival in Canada, the Calgary Stampede, and Expo 86.

DAY SEVEN:
Royals Warmed Hearts in Slave Lake

Brightening Spirits in a Fire-Ravaged Town

William and Catherine specifically asked to visit the Alberta community of Slave Lake on July 6, their day off, a move that surprised citizens of the town. Wildfires had destroyed forty percent of Slave Lake's homes in mid-May 2011, and some residents were still displaced. The conflagration is thought to be the second costliest insurance disaster in Canadian history, with damage estimated at $700 million.

By 7:00 a.m. that day, a line of Slave Lake residents, armed with flowers and Canadian flags, had formed, dying to get a glimpse of the royal couple after they flew in by government jet. There was no doubt that the unscheduled visit by the Duke and Duchess of Cambridge was the best thing to happen to the town in months.

The Miller family hold Canadian flags as they wait for the arrival of the royal couple in Slave Lake.

Above: The Duke of Cambridge inspects a burned-out car, a result of the terrible fire that swept Slave Lake, Alberta, in May 2011.

Right: The Slave Lake fire was one of the worst disasters in Canadian history.

William receives gifts as he interacts with the crowd in Slave Lake.

Royal Titles

Prince William's full title is His Royal Highness Prince William Arthur Philip Louis, Duke of Cambridge, Earl of Strathearn, Baron Carrickfergus, Royal Knight Companion of the Most Noble Order of the Garter, Master of Arts. Quite a mouthful! After her marriage to William, Catherine Middleton assumed the title of Duchess of Cambridge. Prince Charles's full title is His Royal Highness Prince Charles Philip Arthur George, Prince of Wales and Earl of Chester, Duke of Cornwall, Duke of Rothesay, Earl of Carrick, Baron of Renfrew, Lord of the Isles, Prince and Great Steward of Scotland, Royal Knight Companion of the Most Noble Order of the Garter, Royal Knight Companion of the Most Ancient and Most Noble Order of the Thistle, Knight Grand Cross of the Most Honourable Order of Bath, Member of the Order of Merit, Knight of the Order of Australia, Companion of the Queen's Service Order, Member of Her Majesty's Most Honourable Privy Council, Aide-de-Camp to Her Majesty.

The Miller family, natives of Slave Lake, set up chairs and camped out just before 6:00 a.m. Angele Miller, her husband, Wayne, and daughter, Kristin, had been admirers of the Royal Family since the wedding of Diana and Charles.

"We watched the wedding of Diana, the funeral, numerous of the Queen's visits, and stayed up all night to watch Will and Kate's wedding," said Wayne.

"It's part of our history," added Angele.

After the Duke and Duchess landed, they shook hands with many of the thousands of assembled townsfolk, whose grateful faces were wet with tears. Flowers were crowd-surfed across the rows of people to Catherine, who accepted the bouquets with a wide smile and open arms.

Kristin Miller, seventeen, shook the hands of both Royals. The couple even petted her two dogs, Abby and Eddie — a moment Miller says she will remember the rest of her life.

"That was possibly the biggest thing that's ever happened to me," Kristin said, laughing. "I thanked her for the wedding, and she apologized for it being so early in the morning. It's surreal that I just met William and Kate. They're very down-to-earth people."

Catherine, wearing a sleek two-piece suit and wedge shoes, and Prince William, dressed in a navy suit, hopped into a minibus and headed to Northern Lakes College for a two-hour visit. Royal watchers waved flags and

Top left: Skoki Mountain in Alberta was the beautiful natural setting for the royal couple's rest day.

Bottom left: William and Catherine's brief time off was spent at rustic Skoki Lodge.

Love Nest in the Rockies

The Duke and Duchess made a royal love nest out of a rustic lodge in Alberta's Rocky Mountains. After their visit to Slave Lake, the newlyweds spent some quiet time at Skoki Lodge, deep in the Rockies.

The possibility that the couple might visit the area caused a buzz for weeks. "It's in the middle of nowhere," Lisa McKelvie, owner of Trailhead Café, said of the remote lodge.

Some residents said special preparations were made for the royal guests at the popular back-country lodge, with McKelvie saying she heard a cabin had been retrofitted, complete with a bathroom, tub and all. Skoki Lodge's website touts it as "an ideal destination for hikers and skiers ... one can access breathtaking mountain ridges and alpine lakes or explore five different adjoining valleys."

In the winter Skoki, about eleven kilometres east of the village of Lake Louise, is a popular ski-in location, while people visiting in the summer typically hike or arrive by horseback.

"It's good for advertising to [be able] to say, 'they were here,'" said resident Robert Houben.

— *With files from Nadia Moharib and Damien Wood*

In 1860 Albert, the Prince of Wales (later King Edward VII), received greetings from chiefs at a gathering of Natives held in Sarnia, Ontario.

cheered as the Duke and Duchess made their way into the school to speak with emergency workers and residents who had lost their homes in the terrible May 15 wildfires.

Outside, locals packed the streets of Slave Lake, hoisting signs reading: WE LOVE YOU WILL AND KATE. THANK YOU FOR COMING.

At the college the Duke and Duchess spoke with people who had lost their homes. Cathy Redgate and husband, Dave, were among those chosen.

"We showed her pictures of our house before the fire," said Dave after meeting the Royals. "We unfortunately showed her pictures taken during the fire, and she was quite distraught about that. They were just like members of the community out for a little chit-chat."

William and Kate went table to table where residents sat inside the college.

Dave and Cathy agreed the experience lifted everyone's spirits. "This was definitely a nice step out of our [crisis] right now."

— *With files from Jasmine Franklin*

DAY EIGHT:
White Hats in Calgary

The Royal Couple Kicked Up Their Heels at the Stampede

Stampede City's citizens flipped their lids, their pancakes — and their hearts — for William and Catherine when the royal newlyweds choppered into Calgary on July 7 from their hush-hush mountain hideaway.

First stop was the all-important White Hat Ceremony at Calgary's airport. The city's mayor, Naheed Nenshi, performed the honours, and it was official. William and Catherine were the Cowboy Duke and Duchess. Later, at the BMO Centre, Prime Minister Stephen Harper welcomed the couple to his hometown, and Alberta Premier Ed Stelmach also greeted them.

The next day William and Catherine would push the "Plunger" to formally set off the fireworks at the Calgary Stampede. But the official welcomes and ceremonies were really not what this was about. To know what this visit meant to Albertans, you had to wake up and smell the pancakes.

Hundreds of thousands of people had gathered in Calgary for the big parade on July 8. At the Stampede breakfast on July 7 were folks like Maria Grubur, a Calgary woman in her mid-twenties. She was going to get up early on July 8 to see the royal couple. Grubur was too shy to have her picture taken, but imagine her this way: she looked an awful lot like Catherine — and she was about the same age.

And she was thrilled — and impressed — that the Duke and Duchess were in her town.

"I just think they're an inspirational couple," she said as she finished off her pancake breakfast. "We don't get a lot of royalty coming here."

Prince William in Canada

Prince William has visited Canada twice before. In 1991, at the age of nine, he and his brother, Harry, accompanied their parents on a royal tour of Ontario, including a visit to Niagara Falls, and in 1998 both he and Harry joined Prince Charles on a private five-day ski trip to Whistler, British Columbia. William and Harry were given an enthusiastic welcome by young people upon their arrival in Canada.

Grubur said the visit would do good not just for Calgary but for the whole country. "We are getting exposure in Britain and in Europe," she said. "I think it's good to show how great this country is."

And that, in a nutshell, was exactly what this trip was about. Yes, celebrity. But so much more.

It was about service to your country — because that was what William and Catherine had done so magnificently on this trip. Their trek to Slave Lake had summed it up best. Will the fact that they visited that fire-ravaged community change the reality of the devastation people there have suffered? Of course not.

What it did, though, was tell them that people cared. It told them they were important and valued and that the Queen, as Canada's head of state, was concerned enough to have her grandson and his new wife make a detour from an already gruelling schedule to tell them she cared.

We cared. William and Catherine told the world we did. That's why a monarchy is important. It provides a level of state that is above the petty machinations of politics.

William and Catherine were the "It" couple. Everyone wanted them at their party. And guess what? They came to Canada's first.

Top: The Duchess's hair gets caught up in a gust as the couple arrives in Calgary.

Middle: The Duchess is greeted in true Canadian fashion as she arrives in Calgary.

Bottom: A young admirer expresses her warm feelings for the Duchess.

Catherine speaks with Diamond Marshall.

The couple chats with members of the Treaty 7 First Nations.

A Hug to Break Hearts

Six-year-old cancer patient Diamond Marshall only wanted to meet a real "princess" and give her a bunch of flowers, but she was filled with joy as the Duchess of Cambridge bent to greet her. So little Diamond gave Catherine a big hug instead.

"She told me she liked the flowers a lot," said Diamond after meeting Prince William and his new bride on the runway at Calgary International Airport. The Duchess of Cambridge beamed as tiny Diamond ran up to greet her — but instead of flowers, she found herself wrapped up in the girl's arms. Catherine broke into a huge smile and hugged Diamond back.

Her father, Lyall Marshall, helped write the letter that led to the meeting with the royal couple. Diamond, with stage 4 undifferentiated sarcoma, needed a miracle to survive, but for now she just wanted to meet a princess.

The little girl wrote her own letter, saying she was named after William's mother, Diana, and added that her mommy was in heaven with the Duke's mother. Then she wrote that she'd like to meet Catherine and inquired: "Do you want to meet me, too?"

Asked if she thought the Duke was handsome, Diamond paused, then said he was — sort of. "He was a little bit, yes," she said.

— *With files from Michael Platt*

The Duke and Duchess are escorted to the Stampede demonstrations in style.

Prince Edward, Alberta Rancher

Prince Edward, son of George V, and later King Edward VIII, cut a dashing figure and was very popular during the First World War, especially with the Canadian soldiers he served with in Flanders. In 1919 he set out for Canada on an official tour. During his visit, he led the Labour Day Parade and laid the cornerstone of the Peace Tower in Ottawa. The rapturous response the charming prince received was surprising even to him. Edward enjoyed his visit so much that he purchased ranch land in Alberta that he named the E.P. Ranch. He made another official visit in 1927 as well as a private visit to the ranch in 1924. Shortly after becoming King in 1936, he abdicated to marry Wallis Simpson, an American divorcee. After that the couple were known as the Duke and Duchess of Windsor. The ranch was sold in 1962.

Above: The Duke addresses the crowd in Calgary.

Facing: The couple takes in a demonstration outside the BMO Centre.

Prince Edward's charm, exemplified by his smile, proved very popular with Canadians during his 1919 tour.

Because of that, images of Canada, its rich diversity and its (mostly) warm people, were beamed to massive audiences around the world.

We like to think we're the centre of the universe; fact is, we're not. But now the world has caught a glimpse of the Stampede, Green Gables, Quebec City, and Ottawa.

William and Catherine's white hats were firmly on their heads for the Stampede. And our hats were off to both Royals.

Stampede Preview

After arriving in Calgary, the Duke and Duchess got a peek at two of the Stampede's signature events. They arrived at the BMO Centre on the evening of July 7 in a 1912 stagecoach led by the Calgary Stampede Marching Band. They had changed from their earlier, more formal attire into something more comfortable — Catherine in a pair of her own blue jeans and a blouse by Alice Temperley, and Will in a green checkered shirt with jeans and boots.

They had also donned the white cowboy hats given to them by Mayor Naheed Nenshi at the airport. Thousands of adoring fans cheered as William and Catherine were greeted by Prime Minister Stephen Harper and his wife, Laureen, as well as by Stampede president and chairman Mike Casey.

Veteran chuckwagon driver Kelly Sutherland explained the sport to the couple before Prince William was invited to toss the barrel into the back of the wagon. The guests of honour were then escorted to a platform set up outside the BMO Centre near a rodeo pen so they could watch a bull-riding demonstration. After the demonstration, Harper introduced the couple to members of the Treaty 7 First Nations.

The royal couple also met thirty children. Some of them belonged to the mayor's youth council, while others were Calgary Awards nominees or were particularly active in the city. All of them had been selected by the mayor's office to represent Calgary's youth.

— *With files from Jenna McMurray*

DAY NINE:
Wrapping Up the Tour in Calgary

Dreams Fulfilled, Parting Gifts, and Paying Homage

They say there are no do-overs in life — and certainly Medicine Hat senior Frances Miller never expected a second chance to fulfill her royal dream. But seventy-two years after a planning error left a heartbroken nine-year-old old girl clutching a bouquet intended for a Queen who never ended up stopping, she was allowed to rewind the clock.

For just an instant the eighty-one-year-old was that little girl again, finally handing her beautiful bouquet to royalty the way she had practised and imagined all those years ago.

"I never, ever dreamed this would happen," said Frances, moments after meeting the Duke and Duchess of Cambridge.

In 1939 Frances found herself standing on a railway platform, awaiting the train carrying King George VI and Queen Elizabeth. The itinerary called for the train to stop in the southeastern Alberta village, and Frances had been chosen to have the honour of welcoming the royal couple. Bouquet in hand, she stood on the platform, watching as the train approached. But her nervous anticipation turned to dismay as it steamed right on past.

The disappointment felt by nine-year-old Frances, her hair specially curled and her curtsy perfected, was immense. Of course, it was a mistake, not a snub, and when officials at Buckingham Palace learned of it, a letter was dispatched, along with photos of the King, the Queen, and Princess Elizabeth, now Elizabeth II.

William's great-grandfather, George VI, and his wife, Queen Elizabeth, visited Canada's Parliament Buildings during their 1939 tour.

58

Catherine chats with Frances Miller, who finally meets members of the Royal Family after more than seven decades.

Still, Frances believed her chance of actually meeting a Royal had vanished up the tracks forever. Enter Frances's twenty-seven-year-old granddaughter, Kara Meier, who happens to cut the hair of a reporter at a Medicine Hat newspaper. The reporter mentioned it to the right people, and eventually, the prime minister's office got involved.

The result was Frances handing the same type of red roses over to Catherine as she had planned to give to Queen Elizabeth nearly three-quarters of a century ago.

To prepare, Frances was taught again the correct way to curtsy, albeit in a way more suited to eighty-one-year-old knees.

"They're a very beautiful couple, and someday they'll make a wonderful King and Queen," Frances said.

William and Catherine's wedding gift from Alberta was assistance for young people in need. And now the royal couple's parting gift from the province during the last stop on their tour will do the same. Premier Ed Stelmach announced the creation of the $50,000 Duke and Duchess of Cambridge Scholarship, which will see up to twenty-five awards of $2,000 each given annually to post-secondary students who have been in the care of the province and have outstanding academic performance.

The announcement was made at a private reception at the Calgary Zoo's Enmax Conservatory. The couple was greeted by a crowd of eager fans hoping to see them, many with bouquets of flowers. The Duchess wore a satin-and-wool scarlet dress by Catherine Walker along with Queen Elizabeth II's maple leaf brooch, while the Duke turned up in a navy suit.

Strolling by displays about environmental conservation, William and Catherine were given a rundown on carbon capture and storage

Top: The Duke of Cambridge reviews the troops during the final event at Calgary's Rotary Challenger Park.

Bottom: Catherine talks to a soldier during the event in which she and William laid a wreath in Rotary Challenger Park.

technology, the separation process for Alberta's oil sands, and hybrid solar cells. They also met youth who have been helped by emergency shelter funding, which was Alberta's gift to the couple in honour of their marriage.

The massive canvas stretches out to reveal the faces of 155 Canadian soldiers who have died serving in Afghanistan.

The Duke and Duchess specifically requested to see *Portraits of Honour*, and in their final hours in Calgary, they laid a wreath at its base before observing a moment of silence.

Sean Libin is the spokesman for the Kin Canada project, which is the work of artist Dave Sopha. Libin said it was apparent the Royals' interest was heartfelt. "Prince William realizes the personal cost to Canadians to try to bring peace to Afghanistan," he said after briefly meeting the Duke and Duchess at the ceremony.

Currently, there are 155 faces on a backdrop of whimsical poppies. Two more will be added to commemorate the additional lives lost since the artist completed the work.

— With files from Michael Platt, Jenna McMurray, and Nadia Moharib

Artist Dave Sopha with his mural memorializing Canadian soldiers killed in Afghanistan.

The Meaning of a Tour

In his book *Eminent Canadians*, John Fraser has this to say about royal tours: "an enormous amount of effort has always gone into the tours and events the Queen or the governor general [or lieutenant governor] attends. Their presence is often the glorious culmination of years of fund-raising, community organization, and major service commitment. The visit brings honour and dignity to quiet but substantial achievement and volunteer efforts. The pride of accomplishment the local community takes in a royal or vice-regal visit is hard to quantify or otherwise describe in a news story, which is why you seldom read about them, but it is real nevertheless."

EPILOGUE:
They Will Return

What was very clear during William and Catherine's royal tour was that they were two young people very much in love. The tour was planned before William proposed to the then Catherine Middleton. When he announced he would wed, he simply decided to bring Catherine along to introduce her to Canada. What an introduction it was!

Huge crowds turned out to wish them well everywhere. It wasn't just the usual swarms of older people. Plenty of young people showed up, too. Perhaps they were attracted by the royal couple's celebrity, but the younger set also seemed inspired by the Duke and Duchess.

There were so many charming moments on this trip that made us realize William and Catherine really got it. They got Canada. They started to understand who we are and where we're coming from. They now know better than most Britons that we aren't, to paraphrase Homer Simpson, America Lite.

The Duke and Duchess understand that Canada has a distinct and unique culture and that they — and the institution of the monarchy — are among the things that define Canada within North America.

This was a tough test for William and Catherine. The trip to fire-ravaged Slave Lake was especially welcomed by residents.

In a wry moment William asked the group where they would live. "Is there room at the castle?" asked one wag.

The Duke didn't miss a beat and said, "Well, I'll have to check with my grandma, but I'm fine with it."

His reply set the whole crowd laughing.

William made five speeches on this trip. Three — in Ottawa, Charlottetown, and Calgary — were in French and English. In Quebec City he spoke only in French. In Yellowknife he spoke four languages — greeting the crowd in two Native tongues.

His speech in Calgary was personal — emotional, even. He spoke about the 1939 royal tour by his great-grandparents.

"My great-grandmother, Queen Elizabeth, the Queen Mother, said of her first tour of Canada with her husband, King George VI: 'Canada made us.' Catherine and I now know very well what she meant," William told the crowd.

He hit all the right notes. He talked of the "courage and resilience" of the people of Slave Lake as they rebuilt after the devastating fire.

And he talked about the "vital contribution made by Canadians who fought for freedom in the wars of the twentieth century, and by those who have followed their example so bravely in the conflict in Afghanistan."

And he told us they would be back. "Canada has far surpassed all that we were promised. Our promise to Canada is that we shall return," he said.

That was so good to hear. William and Catherine work well together. They are bright, kindred spirits.

They say the whole world loves a lover. Canada, it appears, just loves its royal sweethearts.

IMAGE CREDITS

PAM DAVIES, QMI Agency: page 1.

ANDRÉ FORGET, QMI Agency chief photographer: pages 2 (the royal couple on Canada Day), 3 (the royal couple on their first day in Ottawa), 9, 14 (right), 16 (top), 19 (left), 21, 22, 34 (top and bottom), 35, 36, 37, 38 (all), 39, 41, 42, 43 (top and bottom), 44, 53 (top and middle), 54 (top), 55, 57, 63 (the royal couple wave goodbye in Calgary).

JOHN MAJOR, QMI Agency: pages 6 (the Duchess on the third day in Ottawa), 20, 25.

TONY CALDWELL, QMI Agency: pages 7 (close-up of the Duchess's wedding ring), 14 (left), 17, 24.

CHRIS ROUSSAKIS, QMI Agency: pages 8 (royal couple waves goodbye to Ottawa), 11.

CHRIS WATTIE, Reuters: page 12.

STAN BEHAL, QMI Agency: page 13 (right).

KING LOUIS XIV CANADIAN ROYAL HERITAGE ARCHIVES: pages 13 (left), 51, 56 (bottom).

NORM BETTS, *Toronto Sun*: page 15.

BLAIR GABLE, Reuters: page 16 (bottom).

DARREN BROWN, QMI Agency: page 19 (right).

DIDIER DEBUSSCHÈRE, QMI Agency: pages 27, 28, 29, 30 (bottom), 32.

ANNIE T. ROUSSEL, QMI Agency: page 30 (top).

MARK LARGE, Reuters: page 31.

COMMUNICATIONS NOVA SCOTIA: page 39.

NORTHWEST TERRITORIES GOVERNMENT: page 40.

PHIL NOBLE, Reuters: pages 45 (top and bottom), 46.

LAURA PEDERSON, QMI Agency: pages 47, 49.

CHANTAL TKATCH, special to QMI Agency: page 48 (bottom).

ANDY CLARK, Reuters: page 48 (top).

JIM WELLS, QMI Agency: pages 53 (bottom), 54 (bottom), 56 (top), 60 (all), 61.

LYLE ASPINALL, QMI Agency: page 59.